88 Gratitudes

Always Room for More

Rev. Dr. A. René Whitaker

88 Gratitudes:
Always Room for More

Published by Whitaker Press

Cover design by Kat Stearns and René Whitaker
All rights reserved.

ISBN-13:978-0-9976216-3-1
ISBN-10:099762163X

Dedication
This book is dedicated to the
people who shared their words
of gratitude with me.
You helped me remember
that it is all a gift.

Table of Contents

Introduction

When this gratitude project began, I had no idea how it would impact my life. I wondered:

***What would unfold if
I simply asked people to share
something for which they are thankful?***

The project began as a simple idea to collect some thoughts of gratitude from people. It has been more challenging and more rewarding than I imagined. It has grown beyond my expectation. I continue to be humbled to witness the trust displayed when people were asked to share. Each interaction was transformed by the gift of God's presence in the midst. I decided:

I will call them "gratitudes".

Gratitude soon became the main focus of my preaching. The sermons written during those weeks became genuine responses to these gifts. In the pages that follow, you will discover my attempt to interweave these ***gratitudes*** with scripture that takes us beyond the sermons. May God's grace shine throughout the pages of this book.

Gratitude:
the quality of being thankful

Gratitude:
a readiness to show
appreciation for
and to return kindness

The Gift
Remember the gift.
It is called life.
Too often taken for granted.
When we say, "thank you"
We offer our gratitude.
Is it enough?
What else do we have to give?
I want to be enough
In return for this gift called life.
And if I am not,
May God forgive me
And still offer me grace again today. [1]

---

[1] Whitaker, A. René, *Between Time and Meaning,* [Whitaker Press, 2016], 31.

Chapter 1

Beginning Gratitude

As I begin to put together this amazing book on gratitude, I put my head down and say, "thank you," as I realize what a privileged life I lead. I live with the reality that people share their gratitudes, their joys, sorrows and lives with me, and it is a miracle.

I am surrounded by people who are courageous and resilient. There are people all around me who are creative and generous, kind-hearted and wise. I learn something new about myself and the world every day. Even the tears I shed come from gratitude and joy.

So today I can say, "Thank you God for turning my head so that I witnessed three little girls at the dollar store trying on floppy hats on April 13, 2016." This singular moment changed everything.

Hailee, Kylee and Sadie were their names (yes, their real names). They were just about 10 years old. As I walked by them to pick up a couple of things, I made a decision to ask them to help me start a new project … which would be about *gratitude.*

I hurried to the back of the store where the office/school supplies were kept. I selected a couple of inexpensive notebooks and some colored markers and made my way back to the front of the store. The little girls were still admiring each other in their new-found finery.

Then I set down my items and stepped into the girls' magical world, and asked, "Would you help me start a new project?" They looked at me a bit quizzically. So I continued, "All you have to do is pick a color and write down something you are thankful for. It can be anything. There are no wrong answers. If you help me, I'll buy you each a floppy hat." Well, that sealed the deal.

I'm not sure I can convey the significance of this moment in time. Like many people I found myself feeling unsettled by the increasing tensions that were mounting in our 21st century world. The media in all its facets seemed to be drowning us in negativity. We were too close to hovering into despair. Since I realized I could not change the world, I knew it would be important to shift my own energy. My prayer was that gratitude would lead the way--and it is. Now back to my story.

I AM GRATEFUL

Hailee chose a purple marker and shared:

#1
I am grateful for my family and friends.
Hailee

Kylee chose aqua and shared:

#2
I am grateful for my dog.
Kylee

Sadie chose navy and shared:

#3
I am grateful for my mom.
Sadie

From these simple sentences this gratitude project was born. I paid for my purchases, and the girls each picked out a floppy hat to keep them safe from the summer sun and to be ever so cool and cute as well. (I did give them my card as pastor of the local Presbyterian church ... just in case someone inquired how the hats had come into their possession.)

My last vision of the three little girls was their parading across the parking lot and back into their own lives. It makes me smile every time I remember these few moments. And at times I wonder if they weren't angels from God showing me which way to go.

Even though I didn't choose a marker at that very moment, this was and is my gratitude:

#4
I am grateful for little girls
trying on floppy hats
at the Family Dollar store.

You are now invited to turn the page where you will discover an adventure in gratitude.

I AM GRATEFUL

#5
*For all the great opportunities
that have and will cross my path.*

Alyesha

#6
*I am 17 and pregnant,
but my family loves me,
the baby is healthy
and I am blessed.*

Seely

#7
My family, laughing,

the smell of fresh cut grass.

Mike

#8
*For my boyfriend
who is always there for me.*

Juliana Marie

I AM GRATEFUL

#9

*I am grateful for my children
that keep in touch daily or weekly
even if they live many miles away.
They help with keeping up
our home and flowers
are beautiful all summer.*

Marilyn M.

#10

*You have the power to make it
a great day, for you,
strangers, friends,
and family.
So have a spectacular day!!*

Brandee

#11

For my beautiful family.

Billie May

I AM GRATEFUL

#12
I am grateful for life,
family, creatures,
creation and rest.
LaFern

#13
The grace of God, faith
& answered prayers.
M

#14
I am grateful for the gift
to be able to look
through the lens of a camera
and all things that I otherwise
might miss.
And I am grateful
for all the different people
I have met through photography.
Cindy

I AM GRATEFUL

#15

Springtime, new life,
colleagues & family.

Carl

#16

I am grateful for my friends.
Those I see weekly,
those far away.
We keep in touch thru snail mail.
They give me purpose every day;
at my age it's needed.

Elaine

#17

I am grateful for an incredible
set of family & friends
who have always
been supportive of me.

Matt

Chapter 2
Floppy Hats & Gratitude

Little Girls
Floppy Hats
Sunshine & Hope
Laughter
Connecting with Gratitude
Surrounded by Gravity
Led by grace

Ahhh … we are led by grace.
That's why Jesus says:

"Follow me."

Jesus knew that God is always ahead of us. God is constantly making all things new (see Revelation 21:5). When we feel God's presence, it is always in the midst of ordinary life because we don't have anything else. Sometimes God seems to be speaking to us more vividly than at other times … and yet, this speaking is always in the midst of ordinary life.

When we talk about God in our lives, we can only use the words, images or ideas that we know. When we talk about God in ordinary life, we do so in the middle of a story. Whether we think about it quite this way or not, we stand in the middle of a story about God and human beings. We really don't know anything else, do we?

For Christians, much of the story about God comes to us from the pages of the Bible. Yet, the story of God at work in the world is much bigger and grander than just the parts that are told on the pages of Scripture. God didn't just disappear once the final words of the Bible were recorded. No, God is here in the midst of all our lives today. God continues to create and to recreate the world around us. God continues to be revealed in the middle of life here in 2017 (2018 or whatever year it may be).

Sometimes we seem to forget that God is still in the midst of our stories. How do we meet people where they are and willingly learn about their faith stories while we share some of ours? It seems that too often there is the assumption that people who go to church are people of faith … and everyone else? Perhaps we can search for ways of connecting that assume everyone believes in something.

Here in the 21st century there are many people who don't have a context in which to begin to talk about what they believe. However, Christians do have a context, but I am too often surprised about how distorted that perspective has become.

Yes, Christians are called to follow Jesus. Sometimes this is not easy because we don't have specific directions for where we are going. However, we do have one really broad instruction about how we are to act along our journey. The gospel of John 13:31-34 reminds us of what that one instruction is:

> Jesus said: "Love one another just as I have loved you. By this everyone will know that you are my disciples, if you have love for one another."

This is the one simple and complex rule. It's the rule on which everything else is based. And yet, we keep wondering what we are supposed to be doing in this world. This rule does not say that everyone has to believe exactly the same thing. It does not say we have to eat the same food, speak the same language, sing the same songs or share the same rites of passage. It simply tells us that we are called to accept God's love for us and love one another. That's it. That's the good news.

And because this good news is such a great gift from God, we can keep turning forward to gratitude. It is the only thing we really have the ability to do. When we are thankful for what we have and for who we are, then it becomes possible to love ourselves and others too. It's the only place I know to start in this new creation that God is sharing with us again today.

Today I encourage you to name at least one thing for which you are thankful. Of course, you are invited to list as many as you choose. Perhaps you want to start a space for a visual display of your gratitudes somewhere in your home.

In addition, you might ask someone in your life to share something that he or she is grateful for today as well. Any one at all. It doesn't cost a thing except a few moments in time. But be careful, because it will change everything.

As people shared their *gratitudes* with me, I quickly realized that each one was a gift of faith. With this in mind, you are invited to turn the page, and discover more ways to see God's love at work in this world.

I AM GRATEFUL

#18
*I am grateful for friends
& sunshine.*

Edrye

#19
*For unity ... as Rick said,
"We are all together."
I think that is amazing
& wonderful.*

Gene

#20
*Sunshine, Sam,
Columbian coffee
and the one's who picked it,
friends in this room
and Jesus in the house.*

Rick

I AM GRATEFUL

#21

*"I do not consider myself
thankful but blessed
to be part of this world.
Not only do I thank God
for giving me another day of life,
but for blessing my whole family
with great health.
Every day I look
at myself in the mirror,
and I see not an average person.
I see a person that is determined
to be better than yesterday.
Hopefully, one day I can be
remembered as a person
that made everyone happy."*

Naybert Ramos

I AM GRATEFUL

#22

*I'm thankful for my family,
friends, life, job and that I have
the ability to do whatever I put
my mind to. I am thankful for
my life, family, friends
and good health. I'm thankful for
God blessing me every day
with all I have.*

Mandy G.

#23

*I am grateful to be able
to wake up each day.
Thankful for my job.
I feel extra thankful for
my family. There's always
someone worse off.*

Cheryl

I AM GRATEFUL

#24
*I'm grateful to be healthy
and have a healthy family
and a secure job.*

Evelyn M.

#25
*I am grateful for a family
who loves me and is always
there when I need them.*

Victoria S.

#26
*Who would I be without my sisters
and girlfriends? So much less.
I appreciate them daily
and with passion.
How fortunate and blessed am I!*

Brenda

I AM GRATEFUL

#27

So grateful for good health –
for family and friendships
and for the knowledge that
God loves me – as unworthy as I am
— and that He has a plan for my good.

Carolyn

#28

I am thankful for a God
who loves me unconditionally ...
Who gave his life for me.
And for friends who
listen to my struggles,
who remind me who
I am in Christ.

Serena

I AM GRATEFUL

#29

I am grateful that God
has given me another chance,
over and over again.
In particular, as I reflect on
all my health problems,
I am very grateful to see how God
has healed me and brought me
through all these episodes.
It has also made me realize
that I am truly grateful for each day,
for each day is a great gift
that I have been given.
It also gives me the desire
to make the most of every day,
for we never know
how many more God will give me.
God has blessed me in
so many ways
and for this I am grateful!

Fr. Mark

Chapter 3
Gratitude & Faith

I AM GRATEFUL

#30
*I'm grateful for having such
an amazing job, friends,
person to love and cat to spoil.*
Reanna

#31
*I'm grateful for friends –
the gift to have them,
and sometimes most importantly,
the ability to be one.*
Megan

#32
*I'm thankful for the life God
has given me the chance
to be grateful for so many things.
I'll just choose the big one.*
Jessa

As Jessa wrote: "I'll just choose the big one." For me the 'big one' is my faith. Everything that I believe is grounded in my personal foundation of faith. My first contact with any understanding of gratitude came from this prayer:

God is great and God is good.
Let us thank God for our food.

Of course, when I learned to say this prayer, it wasn't out of any theological understanding of gratitude. Yet, it continues to influence my life today. At times when I'm not sure what else I can or should pray, I remember to say, "Thank you for this food."

For many, faith is grounded in the Christian Bible. Yet, without an informed and careful reading, it is too easy to place our own biases and imperfect wonderings on ancient history. It is good to remember that each of the four Gospels and the other New Testament writings unfolded in the 1st century world which was vastly different than our own. Thus, it is of utmost importance to approach Scripture and what we say we believe with caution. After all we are part of the 21st century world.

Today we know how large or small the world really is. In a few hours, we can drive across the United States or travel to another continent. We are able to communicate around the globe and beyond in many and varied ways. We know that everyone has the same color of blood, and we even know where babies come from. They didn't know all this in the 1st century.

Each morning the sun becomes visible on our Eastern horizon. Every evening it slips out of sight in the Western horizon. We often use the terms the sun rises and sets. Yet, we also know that's not exactly how it happens. And when the sun slips quietly behind the moon during an eclipse, we understand that the world is not coming to an end. How we see the world has changed as the centuries have passed on by.

In 2017 we know how to heat our buildings and air condition our vehicles. We know more about nutrition and food production than we can comprehend. Too we often ignore what we have learned anyway. We are aware of natural disasters that occur in faraway places; and sometimes we can celebrate good news from those places as well.

Yet, in spite of all our knowledge, we often approach Scripture as though nothing has changed since Jesus was born. We seem to forget that God's word is not set in concrete. The Word of God lives and breathes and moves in and among us to redeem and transform the world. The men and women who formed Scripture knew about God even if they thought that the earth was the center of the universe.

The men and women who shared the stories about Jesus understood that the world was a complicated place. They knew that God was bigger than anything they might have imagined. They pushed and pulled at what they saw as an outdated way of viewing God. Over time their perspectives changed. They began to realize that God was more inclusive than they had been taught to believe.

Throughout history women and men of faith have changed what they believed about God. Over time, people have formed and reformed what they believed about God and what they understood about other people too. Of course, all along the way some men and women chose to hold onto more traditional perspectives or perhaps to cling to worn out beliefs.

Like other aspects of life, religious faith calls us to learn new things. When we teach our children the alphabet, we don't stop with **abc**, do we? We help them learn to count higher than **1,2,3**, don't we? It is the same with faith. When we are very young, we may learn to sing, *Jesus Loves Me*. But I would challenge us to add a few more words to that song as we grow up in our faith. So today we can sing:

Jesus loves me and Jesus loves you.
Jesus loves them and those people too.
Everywhere we look around.
We see people Jesus found.
Yes, Jesus loves me. Yes, Jesus loves me.
Yes, Jesus loves me. The Bible tells me so.

So we sing that Jesus loves us. We say that God created the world out of love. Yet, people often forget to act in a way that is consistent with these things. Of course, we are all finite, fragile and flawed. We come to faith with our own limited view of who God is for us. Yet even in the 1st century, Jesus came to help people understand who God is for us. From his perspective, Jesus knew and believed that there was one God who created this world. Isn't that what we say we believe?

We claim to believe that in the beginning God created. We claim that, "In the beginning the Word was with God." We claim that even before the foundation of the world, God loved. And this one loving God sent Jesus to witness to this truth. Isn't this our 21st century perspective?

If we read Scripture with care, we learn that this same God offers mercy and grace for each and every person. However, we also learn that faith in God through the witness of Jesus Christ can provide a new perspective. Sometimes we imperfect people of faith seem to get confused. We may think that God's mercy and grace are created by our personal belief. Then, we worry that people who don't believe like we do are somehow condemned to a life without God's love and mercy.

Yet, it would seem logical that if we believe God freely offers you and me the unconditional gift of mercy and grace, then why wouldn't God offer this same gift to everyone else? And since we have been given this unparalleled gift, the only appropriate response is humble gratitude. We can say, "Thank you, God, for this gift of mercy and grace which is beyond compare."

Perhaps faith is really an ongoing lesson in gratitude. I know that I am continually learning what it means to just be grateful. So today I am thankful to be doing my best to witness to God's truth about gratitude and love. In addition, I'm thankful for the following passage from the book of Ephesians 1:15-17. May it serve as one more marker on this journey:

"I have heard of your faith in the Lord Jesus and your love toward all the saints. And for this reason I do not cease to give thanks for you as I remember you in my prayers. I pray that the God of our Lord Jesus Christ, the God of glory, may give you a spirit of wisdom and revelation as you come to know him."

Perhaps it is this spirit of wisdom that will help us gain a new perspective, and then we can remember to meet people exactly where they are.

And where are we anyway?

We are on this journey we call life.

It is all a gift -- the joys, the sorrows,
the blessings and the challenges.

It is all a gift.

That's why we are on this gratitude-sharing adventure. Once more you are invited to share one gratitude or a whole bunch of them.

You can decide to write them down or lift them up in prayer. Maybe you want to choose a particular color and share something for which you are thankful. The best part is that there is no wrong answer. It is up to you to discover what you want to say.

I AM GRATEFUL

What will you write today?
Will you write just one gratitude?
Or are there more things you want to say?
You can't get it wrong.
It doesn't need to be very long.
Just say, "Thank you,"
and go on your way.

I AM GRATEFUL

#33

I am grateful for my beautiful,
healthy and happy children.
Also, that winter is gone
and the sun is shining.

Angie

#34

I'm thankful for many things,
but something that comes to mind
is opportunity. The opportunity
to do well, to love my family,
to go to school, and to go to work.
So many people worldwide are not
blessed with these opportunities,
therefore, I am thankful for
the chance to succeed, fail
and conquer all the opportunities
that life throws at me.

Bethany Young

I AM GRATEFUL

#35
I am grateful for a lot.
I'm grateful for my parents,
my family, my job, and my co-workers.
I'm grateful every day for every breath
I take. There is so much more
I'm grateful for,
but I have to get back to work.
I'll write more later.

DJ

#36
Something I am thankful for
is my job, my grandpa still being who
he is, and my family being there

for me through everything.

Sarah

#37
I am thankful for being different.

Kyle Lewis

I AM GRATEFUL

#38

*I thank God every day
for the love, support and
spiritual guidance of my parents.
I am also very thankful
for the blessing of a full
tuition scholarship
at the Pittsburgh Ballet
Theatre school.
Time after time,
God blesses me with
the opportunity
to dance in his name.
After struggling with my faith
last year, having the ability and
learning how to properly pray,
I can feel/turn any bad situation
into a good one!*

Jonathan Bright

I AM GRATEFUL

#39
*I am thankful for my family
and you and my customers
and to wake up every day
and have sunshine.*

Lisa

#40
*I am thankful for friends
and family who accept me
for who I am,
through all my faults.
I also am thankful that inevitably
love conquers hate.*

Jordan Boley

#41
*I am grateful for being a Christian,
my family, my job.*

Vera J.

I AM GRATEFUL

#42

*My journey of gratitude began
with the first sensation of
being loved and has blossomed
throughout my life as I have
experienced the beauty and
wonder of this miraculous thing called life.
As the senses of my being became
acute to both my inner
and outer world, an appreciation
developed for even the slightest
sensation. As a child, I was referred
to as Wendy in Wonderland
because I found delight in the most
minute and trivial things.
As I matured and gleaned more
insight and wisdom into both
the marvelous machine that is me
and this all inspiring indescribable
cosmos of which I reside,*

my gratitude for just being alive
to experience –
experience everything –
perpetually overwhelms me.
From the observance of the smallest
cell particle under a microscope
to the images of the universe
I praise the Creator of all things
who has given me sight, touch,
taste, hearing and feeling.
All is truly love,
and I will/shall love
and unfold love, express love
and be grateful
to the ultimate source, God!

Wendy

I AM GRATEFUL

#43

*I am thankful for still being able
to live life and just being able
to wake up every morning
and enjoy each day that I have
with people I wouldn't
be able to live without.*

Taylor

#44

*I'm grateful for my son.
He has made me become the woman
I needed to be. He reminds me
to have patience & take time
to enjoy the little things in life.
He is a constant source of happiness.
Without learning how to love
another person so unconditionally,
I would never have learned
to fully love myself.*

Bekah

I AM GRATEFUL

*The one thing that I cherish the most
in my life, above everything else
in this existence is my family.
I am so fortunate and grateful for
everything they have done for me.
My mother raised me
to be a good person,
and I make it my life's goal
to be able to continue
to hear those words,
"Zachary, I am proud of you!"
She is my hero, and I can only hope
at the end of my life that I know
in my heart that I was a good son,
and that I made her proud.*

Zachary Dale Sweet

Chapter 4
Gratitude for Eloise

#46

I am thankful for my daughter,
a roof over our head,
food in the fridge,
and the beautiful sunshine.

Missy

By this point in the book you realize that a gratitude can take many different shapes. Some are just a few words or a simple phrase or two. Others are more fully developed paragraphs. There are gratitudes from both men and women, as well as people of different ages.

The two gratitudes highlighted in this chapter are unique to the book because they happen to be from a mother and daughter. One of the gratitudes is significant because it came from the youngest contributor. My encounter with her transformed my thinking about gratitude once more.

Eloise was five years old. She was bright eyed and very engaging. Her mom, Missy, worked at Bob Evans. But that Monday evening Missy wasn't working; rather, she was eating supper with some friends.

After they finished eating, Missy brought her daughter, Eloise, over to my table and introduced her. At first Eloise was a bit shy and hid behind her mom. Missy and I chatted a bit, and then they went back to their table.

Missy was enjoying her time visiting with her friends. But Eloise being just five years old got a bit bored. Evidently, somewhere between my table and her chair, she decided it was okay to talk to me. So she caught my eye, came back over to where I was sitting, and, most importantly, she brought a turquoise-colored crayon with her too.

We began our friendship by drawing on the back of the Bob Evan's place mats. Eloise wanted to write her name -- first and last. She had learned how to do that at preschool. Because God's grace sometimes moves in gentle and yet mysterious ways, I happened to have my gratitude collecting notebook with me. So I asked her to write her name in that.

Her signature looks something like this:

#47

Eloise Abams

And it made me smile. Since Eloise had only recently turned five, I didn't ask her to write out an official gratitude. Instead I asked her what her best friend's name was. So I added that fact to her signature page. By the way her best friend's name is ***Julian*** … with a ***J***.

My encounter with Eloise seemed to be the grace-filled working of God's spirit in the midst. It transformed me as I prepared to lead worship for what the church calls *Trinity Sunday*. Just in case you have forgotten, never really knew or have had many other things to think about through the years: Trinity Sunday in the one Sunday on the calendar which is set aside to celebrate the wholeness of God who creates, redeems and sustains life.

Within the Christian tradition we speak of God as Father, Son and Holy Spirit. We talk about the three persons of the Trinity. But this is not equivalent to talking about three human beings.

We use the term "three persons" in order to push at the theological concept that I believe tells us:

> "If God is relational, then we are called to be in relationship with God and with one another. God who is known as Father, Son and Spirit is the same One who creates, redeems and sustains life. This one God cannot be reduced or captured by us … no matter how hard we may try."

This is only one small part of what makes it difficult to define who this triune God is for us. After all the entire Bible is full of stories about people who struggle to talk about God, and it never uses the word or term "Trinity."

The history of the church in the world is filled with so many stories about people who have attempted to describe who God is and how God became visible in their lives, and the concept of the Trinity arose from the midst of all these stories.

Today we continue this struggle of how to talk or write or preach about God at work in the church and the world. It is never very easy to do.

To our detriment, I believe many other-wise faithful people simply ignore or have abandoned the concept of the Trinity because it is so complex. Yet, every time we do this, we consent to making God smaller and more finite than God could ever be.

The doctrine of the Trinity teaches that God is the holy one. God is merciful and mighty. This doctrine tells us that Jesus Christ is our Savior, the Holy Spirit is the one who sanctifies us, and they are one with God who made the heavens and the earth and calls people to new life.

God challenges and encourages. God claims and celebrates. God commands and consoles. God loves and forgives. God asks us to be faithful and offers us hope. God surrounds us with gravity and lifts us up in grace. This is the triune God.

You may be wondering what this has to do with gratitude. Yet, it has everything to do with why this book came to be. This is the framework within which my faith and my understanding of gratitude is built. For me, they cannot be separated in any way.

We stand within God's grace simply because this triune God first loved us in the very act of creation. This is the key. It is simple and complex. In his letter to the Romans, the Apostle Paul grapples with both this simplicity and complexity. Chapter 5, verses 1-5, tells us this:

"Therefore, since we are justified by faith, we have peace with God through our Lord Jesus Christ, through whom we have obtained access to this grace in which we stand; and we boast in our hope of sharing the glory of God. And not only that, but we also boast in our sufferings, knowing that suffering produces endurance, and endurance produces character, and character produces hope, and hope does not disappoint us, because God's love has been poured into our hearts through the Holy Spirit that has been given to us."

Scholars believe Romans was the last letter Paul wrote. It is also his longest writing. Written about 58 AD, it is the only letter he wrote to people he did not know. Paul had planned to visit these newly formed Christian communities, but his life and death unfolded in a different way. So he left those who would follow with the understanding that God's grace in Christ offers both peace and hope.

Without knowing it, Paul changed the course of our history because he wrote to this group of people he did not know. From his discussion of the broad themes of faith, Paul's theology in Romans became the foundation for the Protestant Reformation. It continues to be central for Reformed faith and most of my preaching as well.

Paul is very clear that the message of the Gospel is for everyone. However, Paul knew his first century world divided people into categories (too much like our 21st century world). For Paul, it is only by God's gracious favor and blessing that we have been given life, that we are redeemed by grace and that we will be sustained by hope.

All of life is a gift. While Paul's theology is grounded in the utter necessity of hope and faith, he was not an idealist. Paul saw the world and the people who inhabit it with realistic eyes. He clearly reminds his reader that "all have sinned and fallen short of the glory of God." And he was quick to point out what he saw as contributing to this idea of how people fall short. I'll let you read his rather long lists of shortcomings on your own if you would like.

In Romans 8:31-39, Paul leads us beyond these shortcomings:

"What then are we to say about these things? If God is for us, who is against us? God who did not withhold his own Son, but gave him up for all of us, will God not with him also give us everything else? Who will bring any charge against God's elect? It is God who justifies. Who is to condemn? It is Christ Jesus, who died, yes, who was raised, who is at the right hand of God, who indeed intercedes for us.

Who will separate us from the love of Christ? Will hardship, or distress, or persecution, or famine, or nakedness, or peril, or sword? No, in all these things we are more than conquerors through the one who loved us. For I am convinced that neither death, nor life, nor angels, nor rulers, nor things present, nor things to come, nor powers, nor height, nor depth, nor anything else in all creation, will be able to separate us from the love of God in Christ Jesus our Lord."

So today we too can proclaim, "Therefore, all are saved by grace alone." This is the story of the triune God. We have all messed up. And we all need God's grace to try again and again. Our only faithful response can be to bow our heads or lift up our eyes to the heavens while saying, "Thank you. Thank you. Amen."

I AM GRATEFUL

#48

My 2 children, nice sunny
warm weather, my parents,
my exciting job,
my sister & brother, & God.

Morgan

#49

I am thankful that my daughters,
ages 6 & 11, are getting to
make memories with my 88 year old
grandmother like I have been able to
all these years. She is still very
healthy and active. How lucky are we!
Yesterday we had 4 generations
sitting around the table looking through
100+ years of family pictures.
Every moment of that time
spent with her is a blessing.

Hanna

I AM GRATEFUL

#50

When I think of gratitude
I am reminded
of a passage from Psalm 23,
"my cup runneth over."
My cup is filled with many blessings
from my Mom,
who taught me about love
and acceptance, for my sister
who is a remarkable woman,
for my partner who shares
the joys and sorrow of life
with me every day.
I am full of gratitude
for God bringing my son,
Tyler, into my life,
for showing me
the joy of each day,
the wonder of new things
and that obstacles CAN be overcome.
I am grateful for my friends –
both old and new
who love my flaws and my strengths,
who share this crazy and marvelous
world with me.

Walt P

I AM GRATEFUL

*It is wonderful to be at this point
in my life. I feel so grateful
for a good marriage, good health
and the means economically to support
what I need. Our children are
independent, supportive and
fun to be with.
What more could I ask?*

Dorothy

*I am very thankful for the good life
that the Lord has given me and
also for the wonderful woman
that I have met and am going
to marry on November 11.
I couldn't ask for
a more wonderful life.*

Kenneth

I AM GRATEFUL

#53

I am grateful for the fact
that I am called to prison ministry.
Every time I go into the prison,
people's lives are made better.
We talk to each other.
We share our feelings.
We tell our stories.
It is a little part of a day
when we can be normal,
affirm each other's dignity
and hold each other in community.
I have learned so much from these guys!

David

#54

I'm thankful for
my Lord Jesus Christ,
my family,
my job,
my health.

Tanyell

I AM GRATEFUL

#55
I am grateful for my family.
They are unselfish, giving, loving,
funny, and wonderful!
God has blessed me so much,
and I am grateful.

Crystal

#56
I am thankful for having a wonderful
support group and family that
encourages me to do better
each and every day.
I am thankful for the opportunities
that are given to me
to help me excel in both college
and my social life.
Lastly, I am mostly thankful
for coming out debt free
this year in college, since
that is something not many can say.

Logan

I AM GRATEFUL

#57

*I am grateful that healing always
brings the promise of new
possibilities of life. I am grateful
that life calls us forth to explore
and discover the many secrets
and mysteries that fill the world
with wonder.
I am grateful that the people
who fill our lives bring grace
and the beauty of lives
filled with both pleasure
and pain, struggles and successes,
strengths and the experience of
brokenness that in its turn,
leads us back to healing
– ourselves, each other,
all held in God's love.
Thank you for bringing your grace.*

Charlotte

Chapter 5
It's All a Gift

You wait for us until we are open to you.
We wait for your word to make us receptive
Attune us to your voice, to your silence, speak
and bring your son to us –
Jesus, the word of your peace.
Your word is near, O Lord our God,
your grace is near.
Come to us, then, with mildness and power.
Do not let us be deaf to you,
But make us receptive and open
to Jesus Christ your Son,
Who will come to look for us and save us
Today and every day for ever and ever. [2]

Greed:
intense and selfish desire
for something … wealth, power, food

Gratitude:
a readiness to show
appreciation for something

[2] Oosterhuis, Huub, *Your Word is Near:Contemporary Christian Prayers, [New York; Paulist Press, 1968], 17.*

Not long ago I led an adult study group which took on the task of exploring the seven deadly sins along with their corresponding virtues. It was interesting to discover that there are different lists of these vices and virtues. They vary depending on who compiled them. If you are so inclined, they can be found through the 21st century power of the virtual world. Or you can come up with your own list if you choose.

Each week we discovered new questions and shared lively conversation about the topic at hand. I admit that the idea of including a chapter about one of the seven deadly sins in a book about gratitude wasn't my first line of thought. However, as the weeks and months flew by, it became more and more apparent that one vice seems to stand between us and the possibility of living with gratitude every single day.

Here attempting to block our path is greed. Greed is defined as "the selfish desire for something we don't have." The term "wanting wisely"[3] has been offered as the contrasting virtue. But then the questions begin, "How do we determine whether our desires are necessary and wise or just based on greed?" "Is it possible to discover a definitive answer?" Or are we simply left to wonder?

[3] Meyers, Dr. Robin R., *The Virtue in the Vice: Finding Seven Lively Virtues in the Seven Deadly Vices*, [Deerfield Beach, FL; Health Communications, Inc., 2004], 141-166.

"What is it that helps us determine how to live with the choices we make here in the land of more than plenty?"

Perhaps the following passage from the Gospel of John, chapter 12:44-50, can provide a pathway for our decision-making as individuals and as members of a community of faith:

"Then Jesus cried aloud: 'Whoever believes in me believes not in me but in the one who sent me. And who-ever sees me sees the one who sent me. I have come as light into the world, so that everyone who believes in me should not remain in the darkness.

I do not judge anyone who hears my words and does not keep them, for I came not to judge the world, but to save the world. The one who rejects me and does not receive my word has a judge.

On the last day the word that I have spoken will serve as judge, for I have not spoken on my own, but the Father who sent me has given me a commandment about what to say and what to speak. And I know that God's commandment is eternal life. What I speak, therefore, I speak just as the Father has told me.'"

This Gospel text summarizes Jesus' life and mission. It emphasizes several points which may help us clarify what we are called to believe. In addition, this text offers a pathway to follow for living life here in the 21st century.

In this passage Jesus makes it clear that what he teaches and preaches wasn't something he simply made up along the way. The word that Jesus offered was the same word that God has offered since the beginning. This passage also reminds us that Jesus did not come to condemn the world, but to save the world.

This theme is highlighted throughout the Gospel of John. We may remember words from the 3rd chapter which tell us, "For God so loved the world, that God sent Jesus to save the world." In addition, John's gospel doesn't tell us to love the world "simply because." Rather it calls for us to remember that God so loved the world since the beginning.

Even as God created the world, God declared that it was good. God's own word loved and blessed creation. This creation included us finite, fragile and flawed human beings. Thus, we are called to love the world as we live throughout our imperfect lives because we have been blessed by love.

This is the word that Jesus offers to humanity.
This is the word that will judge us until the end.

At the beginning of this chapter there is a poetic prayer entitled, *You Wait for Us*. It was written by a contemporary Dutch poet and Catholic theologian by the name of Huub Oosterhuis. This prayer guides us toward an understanding of the word that Jesus offers and can lead us away from any place of sin ... deadly or otherwise.

Today and every day the word will come to us. We don't actually have to search for God or God's word as if it is the same as looking for a set of misplaced keys. Think about it. Too often we act as if no one ever witnessed the working of God in the world before this century. People continuously question whether there is a God or who this God might be and what God wants from us.

For 1000's of years people have shared stories about how their lives were transformed by the word of God. This word was spoken and heard in many and varied places. God has spoken through the midst of a burning bush, by the hand of a healing touch, through the rush of a mighty wind and even in the simple words of invitation: "Come and see."

Sometimes this word asks us to go somewhere new. Other times it requests us to share what we have with others. And then there are the many moments when all that is necessary is to change how we perceive where we are. Sometimes Jesus reminds each of us that if we lay down our life, we will be invited to pick it up again in a new way.

Yet in each instance people heard the word of God. In the 10 commandments we find basic rules for living. They were offered as God's word so that we have guidelines for how to live in community with one another. When 10 commandments seemed to be too many, God spoke through Jesus and condensed the 10 to just 2 commandments: Love God, and love your neighbors as you love yourself. We do this because God first loved us. It is all in response to what God has done for us.

Whenever we are called to be witnesses to God's word, we are not selected because we know everything there is to know about God. Rather, people like you and me are chosen because we are willing to begin the journey. For some unknowable reason we continue to follow even when we aren't sure which way we are going.

Thomas Merton, a 20th century Catholic monk, theologian and writer, put it this way:

My Lord God,
I have no idea
where I am going
I do not see the road ahead of me
I cannot know for certain where it will end.
Nor do I really know myself,
and the fact that I think
I am following your will
does not mean that I am actually doing so.
But I believe that the desire to please you
does in fact please you.
And I hope I have that desire
in all that I am doing
I hope that I will never do anything
apart from that desire.
And I know that if I do this
You will lead me by the right road,
though I may know nothing about it.
Therefore, I will trust you always
though I may seem to be lost
in the shadow of death
I will not fear for you
are ever with me
and you will never leave me
to face my perils alone.
Amen. [4]

[4] Merton, Thomas, *Thoughts in Solitude, [New York, Farrar. Strauss & Giroux, 1958], 79.*

Like Merton, we may struggle to believe. We may not always know where we are going. However, we can choose to listen for the word and follow the best way we know how. This word that we hear, this word that we hope to follow is grounded in God's steadfast lovingkindness. This is what we learn in the Old Testament. And this is what we learn as we strive to follow Jesus.

This word can offer us peace that passes all human understanding. We are called to trust in this word no matter what. Of course, there are times when you can't begin to understand what God has been doing. At other times we catch glimpses of God's presence in the midst of it all. Then there are the extraordinary moments when we know that God is present in and among us no matter what.

When we stand grounded in God's word shared through the witness of Jesus Christ, we find meaning in the face of an otherwise meaningless, chaotic and uncaring world. God's word in Christ calls us out of our own self-centeredness so that we have concern for others and this world in which we live. It is a blessing and a responsibility. For reasons known only to God, each one of us has been called to this particular moment in time.

We are called to be witnesses to the reality that the word of God creates and heals. The word of God reconciles and redeems. Again we remember that the stories in the Bible were shared as witness to lives which were formed and transformed by God's word of love.

Each time someone responds to God's call by saying, "*Here I am, send me,*" then God's word goes forth among the people. At that moment a new adventure begins which is grounded in God's steadfast lovingkindness. This word will offer new life, but it may not always be what we expect. Perhaps it never has been.

So we continue to do our best to follow even as we say:

Thank you.

Thank you for the gift of life.

Thank you for the gift of life made new in Christ.

Thank you.

Another word from Huub Oosterbuis will lead us on our way:

We can expect nothing God from ourselves
And everything we have comes from you.
We are dependent on your love and kindness.
Treat us well—do not measure out your grace,
but give us your own power of life,
your Son, Jesus Christ,
mercy and faithfulness
more than we can imagine today
and all the days of our lives.
We are the work of your hands, O God.
You, Lord, have made us and love us.
All our life is your gift,
All your power was in our creation.
And thus you will go on giving us grace upon grace.
What more need we hope for from you?
This certainty – God – is good enough for us.
Amen and Amen. [5]

[5] Oosterhuis, Huub, *Your Word is Near:Contemporary Christian Prayers, 21.*

I AM GRATEFUL

#58
I am grateful for having the Lord
in my life. If it wasn't for him,
I wouldn't have my two children,
my job, my car and my parents/family.
He has changed my life around,
and for that I am thankful
every day I live.

Doreen

#59
I'm thankful for my family and
for the wonderful opportunities
that have been presented before me.
For the opportunity to be able to work
and gain the wonderful education
I'm able to receive. I'm thankful for
the rainy days that make
the sunny ones seem so bright.

Ariel

I AM GRATEFUL

#60
*I am thankful for god and
my communite (sic) and friends and
people watching over me.*

Olivia

#61
*I'm thankful for many things
in my life: friends, family,
my dog, and many more.
One thing seems to
stick out however,
random acts of kindness.
When someone you have never seen
before in your life,
someone whose name you'd
never be able to guess
in a million years
does something for you,
that's what I'm thankful for.*

Gavin

I AM GRATEFUL

#62
I am grateful that my parents
are still here.

Becky

#63
The things I am grateful for
are almost too much to list,
but here goes!
Life
Our Lord
who without him
we would not even exist.
My kids
My family
My dog
For God given me a second chance
for a good life –
and man can it be GOOD!

Kim

I AM GRATEFUL

*There are so many things that I am
thankful for. God has been
so good to me. I didn't receive
the gift of salvation until I was
in my forties, and I am so thankful
He never gave up on me.
Life is still hard, but I can see
God's work in my life and the world.
When I feel despair creeping up on me,
I recall all the many blessings
in my life: my children
and grandchildren
are healthy, caring, loving people.
We are a close family that encourages
and shares all of life, good and bad.
Without the hope I have in Jesus,
this world could really be
a horrible place.*

Debbie

Chapter 6
Gratitude & Grumbling

This chapter changes the the tone of our conversation about gratitude just a bit. Have you ever noticed that at one moment we can offer our gratitude for something; and yet in just a short time, we may find ourselves grumbling about something else?

Have you ever noticed that often they are interrelated? Much of the time this occurs because some part of our experience isn't what we expected. But as we all learn in life, much of the time our expectations aren't quite met. If we can never let go of our expectations, we will surely be disappointed.

For example, we plan a family reunion outside in the park, and the weather changes from sunshine to showers. We expected the weather to cooperate, but it didn't. We can either sit and grumble about the outcome OR find an alternative place to celebrate. After all, the weather is never in our control.

In reality, there is little about life in general over which we have control. Perhaps that is why finding space for gratitude is essential each day.

To help demonstrate the reality that gratitude and grumbling are intertwined, let's turn to a story from the book of Exodus beginning in chapter 15. Here we discover the Israelites wandering in the wilderness. We find the whole assembly of the people rejoicing because they had escaped from bondage in Egypt.

As we share the complex story of the Exodus, we must remember that it is grounded in a particular time and place. In his book, *Strength to Love*, Martin Luther King, Jr. reminds us that, "The meaning of this story was not found in the drowning of Egyptian soldiers, for no one should rejoice at the death or defeat of a human being. Rather, this story symbolizes the death of evil and of inhuman oppression and unjust exploitation."[6]

Reading further in Chapter 16 we discover that the people were not happy with their situation. They were angry with their leader, Moses, and dissatisfied with God. If we can read this story with an open heart, we may come to understand that God really does know who we are. God hears both our gratitude and our grumbling. Perhaps we can never separate the two.

[6] King, Jr., Martin Luther, *Strength to Love*, [New York: Harper & Row, 1963], 73.

To show how they might intertwine, I have included a responsive reading from **Psalm 105** and **Exodus 16**. Today we sit in witness to the intersection of gratitude and grumbling:

O give thanks to the Lord, call on God's name.

If only we had died by the hand of the Lord in the land of Egypt, where we ate our fill of bread.

Sing to God, sing praises to God;
tell of God's wonderful works.

You have brought us out into this wilderness to destroy this whole assembly with hunger.

Glory to God's holy name. Let the hearts of those who seek God rejoice.

God said: "I am going to rain bread from heaven for you. Will you not be satisfied?"

But the people grumbled because it wasn't enough.

*Yet, God brought this people out with joy.
O give thanks to the Lord, call on God's name. Sing praises to God's holy name.*

"O give thanks to the Lord."

Was this one of your first thoughts as you woke up today? Did you thank God before you put on your shoes or had that first cup of coffee? How many of us think "thank you God" for inviting me to come to church again today? How many of us said "thank you God" for transportation to the places we need to go or clothes on our backs, roofs over our heads and food on our tables? Are you able to say, "Thank you, God" because you know there is someone who cares about you?

Right now I invite you to pull out a pen, a pencil, your phone or your computer, and think of eight things for which you are grateful today. If you can't come up with eight, put down as many as you can. Take a couple of minutes to think about this and record them.

I AM GRATEFUL

What are you thankful for today?

67

Gratitude in the form of giving thanks is often neglected in the midst of our daily grumblings. We all grumble (at least to ourselves). Too often we can find a way to grumble to almost everyone we meet. Even as we offer our thanks to God, we are thinking about something that seems to need our grumblings. So now I invite you to list up to eight grumblings you remember from the past week. Give yourself just a couple minutes to record a few of those as well.

GRUMBLINGS

What are my complaints today?

Isn't it true that we can easily think of more than just eight? What is the thing that people seem to grumble about the most? Wouldn't you agree that it's the weather? It is almost always too hot or too cold ... we didn't get enough rain or there's too much snow.

Our health or our healthcare seems to be number two. Today I think that applies whether we are younger or older. We expect our health to always be perfect and our healthcare to cure us of everything at no cost.

Next in line seems to be sports. Why is it we grumble so much about whether some college or professional football team wins or loses (unless you are on the team)? So many people put a great deal of time and energy into simply making a game happen. Can't we just celebrate the fun rather than grumble because they aren't playing the game as we think they should? Just wondering ...

Sometimes our grumblings can make a difference. Sometimes they seem to make us feel better or encourage us to do something. Other times they mire us in misgivings or paralyze us in our misery. I wonder – can grumbling about the weather help us in any way?

Grumbling to our dinner companion about the bad food or poor service won't really help. However, explaining our concern in an appropriate manner to our server may allow us to have a more enjoyable dining experience.

Grumbling because the teacher gave a pop quiz the day we didn't bother to read the assignment won't enable us to pass the class. However, asking the teacher to explain something we don't understand might allow us to learn something we didn't know before.

At times we may find that sitting with our grumblings gives us an excuse to never have to change who we are. If we don't like the food or service at a particular restaurant, we can either choose to cook for ourselves or go some place else.

In most circumstances in life, we can choose to simply grumble OR we can change our actions or our attitude. The Israelites chose to leave Egypt and then wished they had just stayed home. Yet, they continued on their journey into the wilderness. Perhaps we can never be fully prepared for what may lie ahead. Still, we can choose to trust God to lead us on the way. We can have faith that God can provide what we need as we attempt to follow with gratitude.

Are the words we choose today encouraging us to live faithfully before God? Are the thoughts we share showing our respect for others? Do our actions demonstrate that we care for ourselves?

If we choose, we can co-create our world. As we prepare to journey into the week ahead, let's each of us look beyond our grumblings and remember our gratitudes. Then we may remember once more that gravity keeps us grounded so that we are lifted up in grace saying, "Hallelujah, praise God, Hallelujah."

Satisfied

What does it mean to be satisfied?
Are we ever full of satisfaction?
Is it OK to just be satisfied
With what we have or who we are?
So I'm seeking to be satisfied with
What I have and who I am.
We are told that God will satisfy us
But then we keep seeking
Instead of just sitting or standing
Or lying down and feeling fully
Satisfied for who we are
and what we have been given.
So today I will be simply satisfied
And I will savor in satisfaction in God.
Saying a simple *thank you* once again. [7]

---

[7] Original poem, 2017.

I AM GRATEFUL

#65

I am grateful for so much in my life.
All that I have comes from
the Almighty God,
Creator of Heaven & Earth.
I am grateful to serve God and
neighbor as a United Methodist Pastor,
a mother, a wife, a daughter,
a sister, a friend, and as one
with much compassion. I am
grateful as a Pastor to be allowed into
people's lives in a special way—
through times of joy and sadness.
I am grateful as a mother to relive
my childhood through the eyes of
my son and to appreciate the
little things. I am grateful as
a wife to experience a glimpse of
God's unconditional love
through my husband.

I am grateful as a daughter
to see now, as a parent myself,
what my parents did
as sacrifices to raise me & my sisters.
I am grateful as a sister
to be able to watch my sisters
grow into such beautiful women
and see how they love my son.
I am grateful as a friend to share
moments and stories with friends
over a cup of coffee or other beverage.
I am grateful as a compassionate one
to realize how great God's compassion
is for us and to follow that example
when I encounter others. When my
compassion is lacking, I am grateful
that God's (compassion) is sufficient.

Rev. Julie Elmore

I AM GRATEFUL

#66

A wild turkey in my backyard.
Awesome.

Lorie

#67

First of all I am thankful for my life;
many people take that for granted.
I am also thankful for all
the blessings I have had in my life.

Adam Land

#68

I am grateful for God's never-failing
presence, for God's unconditional
love, mercy and forgiveness,
and for God's glorious grace.
I am grateful for God's wisdom
and guidance and my willingness
to continue to listen and learn.

Rev. Carol Ruthven

I AM GRATEFUL

#69
I'm thankful for my children, who,
even though I homeschool them,
teach me something every day.
They've given me an appreciation
for the moment, finding fun,
and understanding others.
Shannon

#70
I am thankful for my family
and friends. My mom for all she
has done for me and her constant
love no matter what. My Daughter,
Bella, for being my sunshine every day.
My friends, for always supporting me.
My wonderful Boyfriend
for helping me through
all of the hard times in life.
Andrea Musselman

I AM GRATEFUL

#71

*I am grateful to have survived this
2nd year of teaching.
So many people listened to me
throughout the year,
and I am thankful for their guidance
and help. God also plays a major
role everyday in the sense that
I am safe, my family is safe
and nothing goes terribly wrong.
I am truly thankful for my job,
my boyfriend, my family and friends.
I'm so fortunate to make music
my career; and even though
I complain, I'm lucky to be in
a country that values what I do.*

Now, this may be cheesy,
but I am also thankful for René.
She listens and provides amazing
guidance and wisdom.
I'm so glad our paths have crossed.
A year ago we were together
around this time and so much
has happened since then
for both of us
(positive & not so positive).
I'm thankful for an unexpected
friend who I always look
forward to seeing.

Katie McDougall

I AM GRATEFUL

#72

I am thankful that I get to make music in my life. I have been incredibly lucky to have had the opportunities to learn violin and participate in so many great ensembles. It's a gift that rewards me every day; and sharing music with the people in my life brings me so much joy!

Anne Rhode

#73

I am very grateful for all my good friends and my wonderful family. God has been good to my family; staying together and understanding each other's problems.

Kay

I AM GRATEFUL

#74

I am very grateful for
the people surrounding me,
my family, friends,
animals, birds, nature.
For the life which is one and only
with its bright and dark stripes
and many more colors in between.
For the talent I was granted from God
and the opportunity to share
this talent with others
and to spread a piece of God
into the ears of the audience.
For my family
here in US and in Russia
who are supportive and loving,
without them I will not be
who I am now.

Andrey

I AM GRATEFUL

#75

I close on a house soon
and it will be great.
Thank you.

VJ

#76

I am grateful for
all the wonderful people
I have been able to meet
and befriend in my lifetime.
I'm grateful for being born
into the family that I love
and care for today; and I am
grateful for the job experience
that I have gained
and the people I've gotten to know
while working and attending
high school. I'm also grateful
for my education.

Abby Licht

I AM GRATEFUL

#77
I'm grateful for
the positive people in my life
that keep me 100%.

Red Hot Robin

#78
What I'm grateful for is being able
to love my family. I was able to
help take care of my mom
until she passed. I am able to
help my dad and try to give him
adventures until his time.
I love talking to my family,
seeing how they are doing,
helping them with what I can.
All of this includes my friends as well.
I get to wake up smiling even
in hard times because of them.
(family & friends)
Thank you!

April Marion

Chapter 7

Remembering
with Gratitude

A Memory

Memories come from many places--
A button, a lamp or even empty spaces.
They provide us a smile or offer a tear.
Sometimes we remember courage.
At other moments we find fear.
We may sing, "Thanks for the memories."
Or wish them away.
A glimpse from the past may cause a shadow today
Or lighten our load in an unforeseen way
Which sets the stage for a brand new grace
And reminds us with care of a loved one's face.
We can share some thoughts with a friend
Or at least maybe two
The tales unfold perhaps more than a few
To remind us of who we once were.
Then they open us up to be more than before.
With shoulders raised high and eyes to the sky
Our hearts and our minds can bid a final goodbye
To what was and what always may be
a memory
of one now truly set free. [8]

---

[8] Whitaker, A. René, *Entertaining Angels: A Guide for Daily Reflection,* [Whitaker Press, 2017], 8.

Rev. Diane Marie Dill, age 57, wrote the following gratitude a few weeks before she died of complications from bone cancer.

#79

I am grateful for my dear friends,
especially René, with whom I talk
every day. I love my family,
Tolly (her dad), Jane (her mom)
who recently died, and Mike (her brother).
I appreciate my education and my fine
creative, sharp mind. I love writing poems,
sermons, short & long stories.
I love dancing around the coffee table
with my 2 daughters,
Courtney and Aubrey (Lanham).
I am grateful for God's grace
for me (& us all) which sets
me free to be loving and kind.
I love praying and teaching people
about prayer. I love teaching God's love.
My life is filled with gratitude & joy.
I am grateful for God's love
for me in the midst of cancer
& crucifixion & for resurrection
for me. Thank you, René, for
letting me share my joy in life.
In God's love, Diane

Fortunately, I was able to travel to visit Diane over the 4th of July weekend. Although her health was failing, we still found time to eat, talk, laugh and cry together. At the time I was in the midst of collecting gratitudes. In spite of her illness or perhaps because of it, Diane shared those precious words of gratitude with me.

When I started this project, I planned to collect at least 100 responses. However, Diane's death on August 3, 2016, sealed the number of gratitudes at 88.

In addition, if we simply turn 88 onto its side, we find double infinity. This seems to be an appropriate metaphor for the amount of gratitude I have for my dear friend, Diane, along with all the strangers, colleagues and friends who willingly shared a gift of gratitude with me. Thus, it allows for the possibility of so much more gratitude in the future.

As with other aspects of gratitude in this book, we now turn to the pages of Scripture. Here we may learn more about why it is important to remember with gratitude.

Genesis 9:8-17

Then God said to Noah and to his sons with him, 'As for me, I am establishing my covenant with you and your descendants after you, and with every living creature that is with you, the birds, the domestic animals, and every animal of the earth with you, as many as came out of the ark. I establish my covenant with you, that never again shall all flesh be cut off by the waters of a flood, and never again shall there be a flood to destroy the earth.'

God said, 'This is the sign of the covenant that I make between me and you and every living creature that is with you, for all future generations: I have set my bow in the clouds, and it shall be a sign of the covenant between me and the earth. When I bring clouds over the earth and the bow is seen in the clouds, I will remember my covenant that is between me and you and every living creature of all flesh; and the waters shall never again become a flood to destroy all flesh.

When the bow is in the clouds, I will see it and remember the everlasting covenant between God and every living creature of all flesh that is on the earth.' God said to Noah, 'This is the sign of the covenant that I have established between me and all flesh that is on the earth.'

This text from Genesis is a significant part of my past, because I was a member of the Order of the Rainbow Girls. Rainbow was established in 1922 under the direction of Mr. W. Mark Sexson, a Christian minister and a Free Mason. For almost 100 years Rainbow has provided leadership opportunities for teenage girls. In addition, it teaches the importance of service to and for others.

Their 1948 guidebook shares this description: "Rainbow is a junior organization for girls of the teen age from Masonic and Eastern Star homes. It also admits the girl friend or chum of the Masonic or Eastern Star home."[9]

"Rainbow is a non-profit, service-oriented organization that teaches girls three basic virtues: Faith in a Supreme Being and other people, having Hope in all that they do, and Charity toward others. The seven colors of the Rainbow are used to represent seven teachings that each member receives on her journey toward the pot of gold."[10]

---

[9] Sexson, W. Mark, *Ritual Order of the Rainbow for Girls*, [McAlester, OK, 1948], 94.

[10] Freemason Information: A Website About Freemasonry, http://free-masoninformation.com/what-is-freemasonry/family-of-freemasonry/international-order-of-rainbow-for-girls / [accessed August 31, 2017].

The Rainbow colors and their associated teachings are listed below:

Red ... Love
Orange ... Religion
Yellow ... Nature
Green ... Immortality
Blue ... Fidelity
Indigo ... Patriotism
Violet ... Service

As a Rainbow Girl, I had the opportunity to do many different things: we visited nursing homes, worshipped in various Protestant churches, and rode on floats in parades. It was fun to wear long dresses for special meetings, but less fun to never be able to wear pants even as the rest of the world became more casual.

I also learned to speak in public, memorizing speeches to go with each office I held. Throughout my years as a Rainbow Girl, I had the opportunity to moderate meetings, participate in service projects, and bake cookies for fund-raising bake sales, oh my! I even played the piano to accompany the singing a couple of times, but that was never my strongest skill.

Over time I learned that Rainbow Girls was less inclusive than other aspects of my life.* It was a difficult lesson to learn. As my college life unfolded, I realized that it was time to move forward and travel down new avenues.

And there have been many adventures along the way: college, seminary and marriage, graduations and new jobs, travel and turbulence, weddings and funerals, fun and friendships, beginnings and endings and beginning again. All these memories are interconnected to make me the person I am today.

Remembering ... we each have memories of the past ... some of them joyous and some not so much. Some memories are part of the ordinariness of life. There are memories we share with a lot of people. Others we may have shared with someone who is no longer with us.

All our memories ... forgotten or not ... contribute to whom we are today. Every time we remember we bring the present to bear upon the past. As we remember, we can reframe it so that we may make new choices in the future.

---

*Since the 1970's the International Order of Rainbow for Girls has evolved to be a more inclusive organization. It continues to provide leadership and service opportunities for teenage girls.

Connections

Connections, connections
Come from many directions.
How do we learn to belong?
Reaching out however we can
Whether we're weak or so strong.
We need to connect whoever,
wherever we are.
Sometimes we are near
Other times they are far.
Pictures of an odometer
from a land far away
Tell us more than words alone
can barely begin to say
What draws us together
Rather than tears us apart
Can we begin by expanding our hearts?
Then we may see how
breath, word or string
weaves us together
Reminding us we are connected
through the Source of all things. [11]

[11] Whitaker, A. René, *Between Time and Meaning, 28.*

I AM GRATEFUL

#80

I am thankful for Family.
Love IS lacking in a major way
in the world we live in today.
But God blessed me with
a big family whose love and
support helped me through
many tough situations.
I am also thankful for family
because when doing ministry
and trying to spread love to others
having a mother and father
plus other family and friends
who are committed to God
makes ministry easier.
My friends and family taught me
the importance of loving others
unconditionally.

Jalen

I AM GRATEFUL

#81

I am grateful for
the people in my life—
those who obviously love me
and those who challenge us—
because each one
presents us with gifts—
some appropriate, some not.
Books are my friends too.
They take me places
where I think I want to be
and sometimes I don't.
They help me to dream and wonder,
and I'm grateful for God
who created all this.

Sr. Mary Jo Toll

I AM GRATEFUL

#82
*I'm thankful for my grandchildren,
flowers, sunshine, visiting
my children & their families.
I really like books! Friends &
lunch dates with them.*

Marge

#83
*I am so grateful that the
Heavenly Father can listen to me
the way He does. Sometimes I am
crying so hard because my soul
is in misery for all the trouble
I have been through.
For a loving Father to listen and
understand even through my sorrow
and tears, is unfathomable.*

Karen H.

I AM GRATEFUL

#84
I am grateful for
the unknown joys of each day.
They come from
so many unexpected places.
A chance encounter
with an anonymous person
and the beautiful connection
and shared humanity ...
a "volunteer" flower or vegetable
plant unexpectedly placed there
by a bird or perhaps a squirrel ...
the thrill of a "musical" performance
experienced with a group of others
and everyone's spirit connected
at the same point in time.
I am grateful for them because
they are gifts from God
and realize they have happened
since time began and will continue
into eternity. They rise above
the trials of each day to bring hope, peace
and contentment. Thanks be to God!

Preston

I AM GRATEFUL

#85

*Thankful that I've ended up living
in this small town where the air
is clean, the fields are nearby,
surrounded by quiet neighborhoods
with small town places and
people to meet again and again ...
at the grocery, book group,
health club, knitting group.
Where I fit in the community
and feel at home.*

Connie

#86

*I'm thankful for the life I have.
Various people have crossed my life
and left their footprints.
It reminds me of "Up With People."*

Diane

I AM GRATEFUL

#87

I am so grateful for so many things
– family, friends, my job, a home
I love and the joy that fills it.
But it is so much more, and I need
to take the time to appreciate
those things on a deeper level.
The family that supports and
loves me as I am, the friends
who have listened to me
in times of trouble and chaos
and prayed for me,
the "many mothers" I have
who treat me as their own,
the co-workers who have accepted me
as if I always belonged there with them
and they have been waiting for me.
They have taught me how to feel
sane again---but all of these things
have been given to me by God,
who continually amazes me
though I should never be surprised.

Stephanie

I AM GRATEFUL

I am most grateful that I have
come to be as free as I am.
I'm pretty sure this freedom has
become strong because I navigated
for about 14 years through
a compulsive behavior disorder illness.
It was truly rough, but each day
almost I prayed "maybe tomorrow?"
And that tomorrow came –
the chains dropped.
I also then was free
enough to meet people in
their innate goodness.
I just wasn't afraid
to meet the stranger,
the person in prison,
the person of another culture,
the very poor street person,
the elderly sick ...
I seemed to have an inner curiosity
that wanted to explore and meet
and come "to know and be known."

I likewise had the privilege
to quit my job and walk
the streets in the inner city
and "come to know."
One other thing has filled my heart
with gratitude –
living in occupied Palestine
in a war zone for 3 years.
Perhaps I came to know
and love the enemy –
at least to a big extent
although some feelings still
get out of shape. I pray I can die
when it's time with
"Thanks, dear God, for this amazing
experience of life!"
Sr. Paulette Schroeder

Chapter 8

Finding Peace Through Gratitude

John 14:23-27

Jesus answered him, "Those who love me will keep my word, and my Father will love them, and we will come to them and make our home with them. Whoever does not love me does not keep my words; and the word that you hear is not mine, but is from the Father who sent me."

"I have said these things to you while I am still with you. But the Advocate, the Holy Spirit, whom the Father will send in my name, will teach you everything, and remind you of all that I have said to you. Peace I leave with you; my peace I give to you. I do not give to you as the world gives. Do not let your hearts be troubled, and do not let them be afraid."

Since it is not possible to address all the ideas presented in this passage, I invite you to look more closely at verse 27. Here we discover just three short sentences which are laden with great meaning:

**"Peace I leave with you; my peace I give to you.
I do not give to you as the world gives.
Do not let your hearts be troubled,
and do not let them be afraid."**

When you hear the word, PEACE, what comes to mind? Perhaps you want to pause right here and jot down an idea.

Does the word PEACE bring to mind a sense of calm, or maybe you think of it as meaning a lack of stress or strife? Is it simply the idea of the absence of war? What kind of peace is Jesus talking about? I would rule out the absence of war because Jesus says, "I leave you my peace. I do not give as the world gives."

We often think that the world would be perfect if there weren't any more wars. However, I'm not sure that is true or humanly possible. I also don't think that the sense of peace in this instance means calm and placid. After all, a constant calm and placidness would soon become stagnant and stale. Here I invite you to picture a completely still pool of water. In the worst sense, calmness equals motionless which then would be the equivalent of death.

In this context could PEACE mean "equanimity," "mental calmness" or "composure in the face of a difficult situation"? If so, this can begin to draw us closer toward what Jesus was pointing. However, we need to take his cultural context into consideration. His understanding of the word PEACE would come from the Hebrew word SHALOM, which points to an attitude of peace in the wholeness of life. Jesus would call us to a space of "right relationship" with God, ourselves and other people.

A traditional blessing for peace might include: "May your life be filled with health, prosperity and success." These are the types of attributes that we could hope for ourselves and others. However, we still hear Jesus saying, "I leave you *my peace*. Not as the world gives, but as I give."

So in this case peace does not necessarily mean an absence of war. Neither is it simply an absence of strife nor even an absence of stress. This is because human life is filled with all these things. And people aren't always calm in the midst of life's many challenges. Some situations require us to answer with passion and unsettledness, don't they?

Perhaps Jesus' sense of peace calls for us to listen for God's word in the midst of stress and strife. It calls for us to hear what is being said and to respond in an appropriate way.

Sometimes it is right to call for peace and quiet. Sometimes we have to kick the dust off our feet. Sometimes the tables must be knocked over to emphasize an important point. As we are all aware, some situations require tears. Others call for laughter. Then there are those moments which seem to insist on cries lost in the wind. The Bible itself reminds us that there is a time and a season for everything under heaven.

So today I offer this definition of peace:

**Peace is the ability
to face life's challenges
as best we can
in a manner
that is appropriate
for a given situation.**

Plus gratitude.

If we stop and think about it carefully, gratitude requires us to go into and even beyond the situation we find ourselves in and say:

Thank you God.

**Thank you for something
in us, around us
OR
directly in front of us
on the path.**

Whatever our day brings, there is something for which we can be grateful: a person, a place, a memory, a basic element of life such as water or air. Sometimes we can be grateful for some small convenience or a nudge from somewhere. Sometimes we can look up and see the stars ... or we can look ahead and see a possibility ... or we might look around us and find beauty. Perhaps even in our dark moments of grief or despair we might be able to breathe the word, "thanks." And that will be enough.

"Thanks." Such a simple word filled with great meaning. When we stop and share a gratitude or speak of something for which we are thankful, we change our perspective.

This is why I began collecting gratitudes from other people. That is why I have written this book. My hope is that if we each begin and end our day with gratitude, the entire world can be changed for the better. This is also why I am grateful for little girls in floppy hats. For they helped start this endeavor. I am also grateful for all who have shared their words of gratitude with me.

Saying a simple word of thanks is always a helpful reminder that we haven't done any of this by ourselves. Not one thing is of our own making. Even when we are disgruntled by where something has come from, we can understand that we didn't create it. It is important to realize that we simply cannot make something out of nothing.

With this realization we may come to understand that the opposite of gratitude isn't ingratitude. Rather the opposite of gratitude is forgetfulness. It is all too easy to forget that there is always something beyond ourselves. There is something more than this one moment in time.

When we share our gratitude, then we remember. In this sharing, we can help others to remember too. And it does change everything.

What are you grateful for today? The gifts of gratitude are beyond measure. When we share the gift, we can discover peace again and again.

One thousand gifts
Almost too many to list
One thousand gifts
Just one at a time.
Not too fast to collect
Not too slow to let go.
One thousand gifts
Not too many to know
But collecting them slowly
Is a hard thing to do.
I want to acknowledge
The gift of what's true.
My heart ebbs and flows
Relearning what it knows
That the gifts keep
On giving from zero
To beyond one thousand
Plus one and then
With gratitude for what will be
And what has been.
We can bow our heads,
With a "Thank you" and Amen.[12]

---

[12] Original poem, 2017.

I AM GRATEFUL

What are your gratitudes for today?

About the Author

Rev. Dr. A. René Whitaker is an ordained Presbyterian minister. She has worked with congregations in transition for 20 years. Rev. Whitaker earned a Master of Divinity at Austin Presbyterian Theological Seminary. In 2014, she completed a Doctor of Ministry in Science and Theology at Pittsburgh Theological Seminary. Her final project is entitled, *Creating Community in a Networked World*.

Rev. Whitaker is available to lead retreats, preach and offer spiritual care. In 2017, she completed *Entertaining Angels*: *A Guide for Daily Reflection*. Other books include: *Gravity, Gratitude, Grace: A Journey of Healing & Hope* (2012) and *Between Time and Meaning* (2016).

46628769R00065

Made in the USA
Columbia, SC
29 December 2018